Before Your Last Breath

Your Spiritual Transition
and End-of-Life Planning

Jilliana Raymond

Before Your Last Breath:
Your Spiritual Transition and End-of-Life Planning

Copyright © 2019 Jilliana Raymond

Published by
Aviva Publishing New York

Book design by
Deborah Perdue, Illumination Graphics
www.IlluminationGraphics.com
Call 541-862-7021 or email
deborah@illuminationgraphics.com

Author photo by Claire Hageman

Editor: Beth Cooper, Professional Proofreading Plus
www.professionalproofreadingplus.com
professionalproofreadingplus@gmail.com

Softcover ISBN: # 978-1-947937-22-2

Library of Congress Control Number: 2019905894

Dedication

Inspiration ignites a journey. Implementation of a successful project can depend on a dedicated team working in coalition to achieve a goal. Not only have I been guided by spiritual forces that provide life wisdom and inspiration but I have been surrounded by a support network of proficient individuals who have been instrumental in the creation of this work. Thank you to Deborah for your incredible design, Dar for contributing to the valuable content, Beth for your superior organizational and editing expertise, Susan for making this project possible, and Jane for believing in the compilation of this work.

Table of Contents

Section III
What to Do When Faced with a Terminal Illness

Section IV
After Death Procedures
Information to Share with Your Loved Ones

Section V
Resource Tables

End-of-Life Worksheets

Preface

For many years I have been teaching my students that the life we experience on earth is a mere breath in relation to the life we experience in our spiritual domain. While our beliefs largely determine how we experience our spiritual life, what we do during our physical life contributes to our individual soul expression. Death is not an end, but a new beginning.

My first experience with death was more than fifty years ago with the passing of my grandmother. She suffered a stroke and was cared for in our home until her crossing. I wouldn't hear from this matriarch for another twenty years with the passing of my mother.

At the time of my mother's transition from this life, I didn't have the resources to be at peace with her passing. I entered a deep depression that took months for me to rebound. Simultaneously with my mother's departure, I faced a significant life disruption with the separation of my marriage. Although my grandmother and mother were no longer of this physical world, they would both guide me through this difficult time and help bring me the peace to move forward.

My grandmother's guidance would come to me through the intervention of an intuitive. The intuitive had no previous access to the information that was provided. I will admit I initially questioned the logic and rationale of this encounter. This would be my first connection with life beyond. The interaction provided me significant solace and initiated my curiosity to discover more about life beyond our physical reality and the spiritual aspects of our living dimensions.

I did not need an intuitive to connect with my mother. I remember waking one night to see the image of her floating into my room. She wore a chiffon green gown, exuded the youth she expressed in her wedding picture, and offered me her broad inviting smile. Her voice was sweet and reassuring. She came to inform me all would be fine. Her presence was fleeting. This experience was all new to me, and I questioned my sanity. But that was my mother, the individual that I'd trusted all my life, and I was quite sure I wasn't experiencing a hallucination. This encounter rekindled my desire to explore more deeply into the spiritual world that defines our being.

My observations, interviews with medical personnel, and my own encounters with individuals in transition have proven to me that life exists beyond our physical experience. How one experiences their existence after their physical life is determined individually by the life foundation they have encountered. While every individual's passing is unique and experiences variable, transition brings peace and renewal to the life that has been challenged and is in decline. There are too many researches who have documented countless depictions of afterlife interactions to ignore the seeming hallucinations of a person in transition.

Dr. Kubler-Ross, a noted American-Swiss Psychiatrist, presented the concept of the five stages of thinking of the terminally ill patient. In her documentation she acknowledged that denial, anger, bargaining, depression, and finally acceptance accompanied most individuals given that fateful prognosis. Her documentation included the emotions and experiences of over 20,000 clients. She indicates in her book *On Death and Dying*, "There are two certainties in life . . . that we are born into our life from spirit, and we will return there."

Dr. Brian Weiss, another noted psychologist and hypnotherapist, documented many case studies in his title *Many Lives, Many Masters*. Through countless past life sessions Dr. Weiss indicates that by exploring previous life trauma through hypnosis, the past life encounter was instrumental in providing resolution to a current life scenario.

Noted psychologist and hypnotherapist Dr. Michael Newton, documented client resolutions through his works, *Journey of Souls* and *Life Between Life*. And Dr. Raymond Moody, psychiatrist, physician, and author explored life after death through his case studies of near death experiences (NDEs) and patient encounters. His work is presented in his book *Life after Life*. These and other experts are lending credibility to the realization that human life is much more than a singular experience. This realization alone should bring immense comfort to any who have suffered through the loss of an important loved one or alleviate much of the concern one can experience watching the decline of a beloved individual, knowing that life is a transition from one dimension into another. Questions will arise regarding the afterlife/between-life experiences. This is where continued research and discussion needs further exploration.

In my quest to learn more about death and dying, I attended End-of-Life Doula training through INELDA. INELDA, and other end-of-life organizations, invest in providing dignity, emotional support, and provide assistance in organizing final life details. Individual care programs can be designed to meet the needs of the person preparing for transition, including bedside vigil to relieve fatigued family members during final days. Doula care is designed to work in conjunction with medical professionals including hospice personnel.

Doula care can be initiated when an individual is no longer able to care for themselves. Hospice care can be initiated generally once curative measures have shown no improvement, usually six months prior to an anticipated life departure.

While doula training covered most aspects of supportive

care through the end-of-life process, I realized that the topic of afterlife exploration was never addressed. Because of my own life experiences and my spiritual ministry training, I wanted to present a different concept of death; one not of fear but instead an inviting image of an awaiting spiritual life. All of us are so much more than the physical suits we identify with during our physical life phase. I know that we will all transition to our spiritual house, one filled with love, peace, and the welcoming arms of those who have gone before us. Through this book, I wish to share a vision of the peaceful spiritual transition of renewal that awaits us all.

How to Use This Guide

First and foremost, this book includes a discussion of continued conscious awareness of the soul's journey beyond one's physical residence. In the preface, you will find my reasons for bringing this dialogue to the forefront, and discover some of the research done on life beyond our physical reality. In addition to discussion on afterlife potentials, is a detailed practical planning guide for life transition, as well as a listing of resources for medical directives, medical treatment options, burial preferences, and funeral cost comparisons. To help organize personal financial papers, included worksheets provide one collective source to document contact information.

Section I addresses every individual's spiritual core and allows individuals to review their life interactions.

Section II is designed to assist individuals in making important decisions on final life affairs well before any anticipated transition. This section also addresses funeral options and financial account considerations.

Section III discusses all matters concerning individuals faced with a terminal prognosis. It includes reference tables that identify who can legally pronounce death, current legal death protocols by state, sample Death

Certificate and contact resources for IRS, Social Security, and Veterans Affairs Administrations. Worksheets can be utilized to list credit vendors with contact information to be easily accessible for individuals assigned with the responsibility of resolving final financial affairs.

Section IV deals with all final protocols associated with after death finalization.

Section V includes reference tables and worksheets to assist with organization and decision-making.

Finally, this book empowers an individual to be the designer of their personal transition process by first informing the reader of the process and by alleviating concerns surrounding transition planning.

Section I

A Spiritual Transition

By Spiritual Design

*W*e are all spiritual by our very nature. No matter what spiritual foundation provides meaning in our life, every living soul originates from the spiritual realms. What happens during our physical life is largely determined by our individual creative direction and the life influences determined by our social exposure. This is usually influenced by the belief systems that have been integrated into our life and by the choices that we make through the varying challenges and experiences that have been encountered. What happens in your spiritual world largely depends on the choices you make during your physical life, your belief system, and the creative exploration realized during any physical journey.

When your soul is called to return to its spiritual home, designated members of your spiritual family (not always those individuals of your immediate physical family) will guide your soul back into the spiritual domain. Your soul will be greeted by departed family members, trusted friends, spiritual guides who have accompanied you throughout your life journey, along with an assortment of angelic beings that will help provide comfort and reassurance as your soul reenters the spiritual labyrinth.

Every individual has a personal guiding spirit that has been with them since birth. Your guide assists in providing steerage throughout your life and is often most notable as that whisper in your ear alerting you to either reconsider a thought or applaud you on a job well done. Once you have traveled into the spiritual dimension and have had a chance to process your return home, your guide (at a moment designated by you) will escort you through a panoramic private review of your life. You will revisit the emotional imprint you created during your physical life by reviewing individual encounters. You will become aware of every accomplishment, and you will assess less complimentary interactions you could have handled differently. You will be able to determine what course you will take to balance a complicated interaction and note which areas during your life experience you would like to revisit or resolve.

It is important to note that there is never any judgment from any spiritual resource. You stand alone as the guardian of your life activity. There is accountability for all actions, but how, when, or if you wish to address any resolution is up to you. While you may choose to postpone resolution of any compromising emotional impact created during your life, you will eventually want to resolve past conflict to be able to expand your soul's evolution.

In addition to a review of your current life you will have access to all timelines and have unlimited access to all wisdom and knowledge. Most importantly, you will reengage with members of your soul family and those friends and associates who are close to you, even those you may not have been aware of during your physical residence.

Just as you were the creative designer of your physical life, you now become the designer of your experience in your spiritual house. You may choose to resume the field of interest you pursued in your physical house or choose something entirely different. Imagine being able to explore unlimited activities of interest. There are a myriad of roles of service to employ, scientific research to conduct, universities to attend, artistic pursuits to engage in, concerts to relish, instruments to play, choirs to join, athletics to pursue, games to play, places to travel, and social engagements to enjoy. Removing the physical clothes you wore during your earth life reveals the essence of the spiritual master: your true identity. You might consider transition from the physical world as a graduation into your spiritual house. Death is not an end but a new beginning.

"I am ready to meet my Maker. Whether my Maker is prepared for the great ordeal of meeting me is another matter."

— Winston Churchill

You Are a Living Legacy

Create a living history. Many individuals consider their life history as routine and ordinary. Make no mistake there are no ordinary souls, only individuals doing extraordinary things. While some individuals have received more notoriety than others, there are no ordinary lives. It is time for you to consider how you may have inspired someone in your life or perhaps someone inspired you. There may be details your loved ones would appreciate learning about you, an observation you had, a challenge you've overcome, or a memory you never shared. Before your life memoirs are silenced, take time to tell that anecdotal story, provide some history for those you leave behind, or provide that important recipe. Create that memory for those you leave behind to remember about you. If there are pictures or memoirs, have you identified the significance of these? Is there a specific ancestral lineage you never shared or a story of your grandparents you found specifically endearing? Now is the time to record these final reflections.

Resolving Unfinished Issues

There is no better time than the present moment to resolve unsettled issues. This may be the apology you could never make, or the thank you that you never had time to send. You may want to express that belated sympathy, or tell someone how cherished they have been in your life. Forgiveness is the key to lighten the emotional burdens absorbed during lifetimes of limitation. It is much easier to resolve issues while in the physical plane than to wait to resolve conflict from the spiritual realms. Final thoughts may be written or presented as an audible message. As you prepare to leave your current physical world, leave all the accumulated unresolved history behind.

Honoring Your Beliefs

It is time for you to honor your own beliefs instead of worrying about the agenda of others. Create the emotional and spiritual support that will sustain you through your transition. You can surround yourself with treasured items or recreate your favorite environment within your room to help support your emotional senses. This is the time to indicate how you wish your final time to unfold.

Death is Not an End but a New Beginning

*W*hile every individual's passing is unique and experiences variable, transition brings peace and renewal to the life that has been challenged and is in decline. There are too many documented depictions of afterlife interactions to ignore life continuance.

I have interviewed individuals who have had near death experiences. Each individual reported being immersed in an incredibly loving environment. Some of the individuals were given choices whether they would continue their physical journey and some were encouraged to return, providing them with a window into their future physical adventure. For most, the encounter provided them with sufficient support to continue living a life that mattered, and the peace of knowing what would be waiting for them upon their return. The experience also left most of these individuals profoundly changed emotionally, more at peace with an indescribable serenity about all life matters.

Imagine an environment of pure love, where infinite possibilities await. Imagine a place where there is no hate, no judgment, no pain, where harmony pervades, and learning is freely available. This is the essence of the spiritual domain. This is where all return to and the domain where all reside in between a physical existence. You have an opportunity to assure those you love that you will merely step through a portal into another dimension. Let them know you will be aware of their personal challenges, and that you will be present at every celebration. You will hear their thoughts and be aware of every prayer. Tell them to dry their tears as best they can, and to celebrate the life lived and the loved shared.

J.R.R. Tolkien states "End? No, the journey doesn't end here. Death is just another path, one that we all must take." And in the words of Edgar Allan Poe "the boundaries which divide Life from Death are at best shadowy and vague. Who shall say where the one ends, and where the other begins?"

Physical life is merely a temporary experience. No one ever loses those that have been loved. Those who have gone before us surround us with their love. Death is not an end. It is a return to a spiritual residence.

*"It is the secret of the world
that all things subsist and do not die,
but retire a little from sight
and afterwards return again."*

— Ralph Waldo Emerson

What to Expect
in the Spiritual Realms

*I*magine an environment of pure love, where infinite possibilities await. Imagine a place where there is no hate,
or pain; where learning is freely available and energies exist in
harmony. Whatever endeavor fuels your passion is available.

The question might be, "what do I want to experience
in my spiritual world?" Your beliefs will largely govern what
you experience after your transition. Strong beliefs shaped by
religious or cultural teachings may influence how you transition into the spiritual dimensions and may influence your
interaction once you've returned to your spiritual home.

If you've lived life on the fringe of society or have felt
your life unfairly limiting, this may influence your transition.
If you harbor deep hatred, regret, guilt, or blame, take time
now to resolve those feelings so that you may be free to peace-
fully transition into the arms of an unconditionally loving

dimension. Be assured there is no council of elders standing in judgment of any life scenario other than your soul awaiting your own assessment of your accomplishments or regrets. There is no council of elders waiting to dole out some anticipated punishment. There is no hell, other than that which is created in your mind. There is no declared resolution for any of your interactions, other than the accountability designated by your own soul.

As you begin to incorporate more of your spiritual essence, your spiritual dimension will emerge. While there are similarities for most reentering their spiritual home, you will most likely experience a reunion with those beloved members of your family who have made the journey before you.

Not so long ago, I sat with my father during his transition. He had a good life, but in his aged years he was definitely embracing his own transition. Shortly before his passing he engaged in conversation with familiar individuals who had transitioned before him. With a wide smile across his face, he waved to these otherwise invisible individuals, asking someone to fix him a Scotch, another to get him his cane and remarking he hadn't seen this person or that person in such a long time.

This story is similar to the recordings nursing and hospice personnel have witnessed during their careers as health practitioners.

Once you fully integrate back in to your spiritual house, you will find unlimited opportunities to pursue. This may include goals and interests you were unable to complete during your physical life due to unexpected challenges or limitations. You become the spiritual designer in your spiritual world. There is a wonderful statement..."As above, so below." Life is a continuum but without all the restrictions, ailments, and physical compromise too many experience in their physical environment.

Section II

Making Important Decisions

Making Important Decisions

*T*here is one certainty all of us must face: that all life will at some point exit the physical world and return to a spiritual plane. The topic of death is a subject few honestly address, but it is a topic that needs to be discussed. How each of us will experience life transition will be individual. This can be a much easier process with some pre-planning. There are certain truths and practical measures all can employ to provide for a smooth transition from this physical plane into the spiritual dimensions. There are, of course, final expenses and financial details that will need to be addressed. All of us need to communicate honestly to our families how we would like others to respect our final wishes, and all of us need to be responsible for resolution of personal affairs that have accumulated during our physical life phase.

Creating a Living Will

Creating a living will is a way to ensure your individual requests are honored. If you do not already have a will of record, it is advisable to create one. While putting your thoughts together you will need to determine how you wish to disperse any personal property you don't believe any family member, close individual, or organization may want to take possession of. If you are not using legal counsel to create your will, you will need to determine if your state requires your will to be on file. Notarizing a home-created document of your final wishes will normally suffice under state scrutiny. Be sure designated persons delegated as executors have a notarized copy of your will or have quick access to the document for the executor of your estate. You will need to state clearly if organ donation is desired within the will's content along with burial option, especially if the body is to be donated to science for research purposes.

Remember, as life changes, your will may also require change. It is important to review your will as needed to ensure your final wishes are honored.

If an individual were to transition without a document of intention or "will," state law may determine beneficiaries and act as administrator of your estate. Each state's laws may differ, so it is advantageous to be aware of your state's protocols to assist you in determining how you wish to have your estate handled. You can review legal trusts via the web or create a living trust for a nominal fee. Visit **www.LawDepot.com.**

If you have holdings (usually over $500,000) that would create an estate, you may want to consult legal counsel to create a trust. See following Sample Advanced Life Directive. Note: Free forms can be obtained from **FormsSwift.com**. **Place Advanced Directive in the Google search bar, and apply your specific state to obtain free forms.**

North Carolina maintains an Advance Directive Registry. By filing your advance directive with the registry, your health care provider and loved ones may be able to find a copy of your directive in the event you are unable to provide one. You can read more about the registry, including instructions on how to file your advance directive, at http://**www.secretary. state.nc.us/ahcdr/Forms.aspx. 5.** You may also want to save a copy of your form in an online personal health record.

Creating a Trust

- **Estate Planning**: If you have any properties you wish to dedicate to specific individuals, you may wish to investigate drawing up a legal trust. This will ensure that designated properties will be distributed to the select recipients. For instance, if leaving an endowment for a child or grandchild, distribution of assets can be detailed in scheduled increments, at age of maturity, or designated for specific use and are generally transferred to specified accounts tax free. Other properties can be detailed as part of your living will as well.

- **Assignment of Estate Executor**: An estate executor is usually implemented to assign responsibility to an individual who will be responsible for intervening on behalf of your real estate, boat, or tangible sale of assets. The estate executor will also address any outstanding debt resolution and dispersal of any final estate funds to designated vendors/recipients. In addition, the estate executor will be responsible for the final accounting to the IRS.

- **Assigning Power of Attorney:** The power of attorney can serve dual functions as the estate executor and power of attorney. The power of attorney is given legal authority to sign contracts, pay bills, and negotiate on behalf of an individual who is no longer able to make decisions on their own.

Practical Planning

Before anyone is faced with life passage, practical preparation should be undertaken. This can be done well in advance of any presenting diagnosis.

Creating Medical Directives

It will be necessary for you to understand the differing medical directives so you can be well-informed and proactive about your final desires.

A. DNR Order: DNR stands for Do Not Resuscitate. This medical directive instructs an ancillary caregiver, EMS, or other medical personnel not to initiate CPR should heart function cease.

B. DNI Order: DNI stands for Do Not Intubate. This medical directive means that chest compressions and cardiac drugs may be used to stabilize your medical condition, but no breathing tube can be placed.

C. DNH Order: DNH stands for Do Not Hospitalize. This is a lesser known medical directive.

D. Feeding Tube: Determine if you would ever want artificial nutrition through a feeding tube.

E. Artificial Respirator: Determine if you would want to be on an artificial respirator.

F. Research: Determine if you want your body donated for research. In this category, pre-arranged notification will need to be made.

All orders must be signed by a physician or authorized caregiver. All orders must be available and presented to EMS personnel, hospital attendants, funeral personnel, and/or legal authorities upon request.

Advance Directive Sample

NORTH CAROLINA ADVANCE DIRECTIVE
My Desire for a Natural Death

I, _____
PRINT YOUR NAME
Being of sound mind, desire that, as directed below, my life not be prolonged by
life-prolonging measures:

1.   When My Directives Apply
My directions about prolonging my life shall apply IF my attending physician
determines that I lack capacity to make or communicate health care decisions
and:

NOTE: YOU MAY INITIAL ANY AND ALL OF THESE CHOICES.

_____I have an incurable or irreversible condition that will result in my
death within a relatively short period of time.

_____I become unconscious and my health care providers determine that,
to a high degree of medical certainty, I will never regain my consciousness.

_____I suffer from advanced dementia or any other condition which results
in the substantial loss of my cognitive ability and my health care providers determine that, to a high degree of medical certainty, this loss is not reversible.

2.   These are My Directives about Prolonging My Life:
In those situations I have initialed in Section 1, I direct that my health care providers (initial only one):

_____MAY withhold or withdraw life-prolonging measures.

_____ SHALL withhold or withdraw life-prolonging measures.

I Want this Directive to be Effective Anywhere I intend that this Advance Directive
be followed by any health care provider in any place.

I have the Right to Revoke this Advance Directive I understand that at any time I
may revoke this Advance Directive in a writing I sign or by communicating in any
clear and consistent manner my intent to revoke it to my attending physician. I
understand that if I revoke this instrument I should try to destroy all copies of it

WITNESSES

Witness 1 name: _____

Date: _____Witness Signature: _____

Witness 2 name: _____

Date: _____Witness Signature: _____

NOTARY PUBLIC COUNTY, STATE

_____COUNTY, _____ STATE

Sworn to (or affirmed) and subscribed before me this day by
_____   _____

(type/print name of declarant)

_____   _____

_____   _____

(type/print name of witness)   (type/print name of witness)

Date: _____   _____
(Official Seal)   Signature of Notary Public,

_____Notary Public

(Printed or typed name)

            My commission expires_____

Choosing Your Burial

*Y*ou can arrange your funeral in advance. Funeral homes will walk you through the process and help you choose the modality that is right for you. Funeral homes will generally coordinate all details surrounding death processing, alleviating much of your family's concerns during a difficult transition period. Should a home service be the chosen modality for your final goodbye, you may still require the assistance of a funeral home to provide cremation or burial services on your behalf.

Home burials are not legally sanctioned in most states. However, there are currently a few states (New York being one) that allow home burial on personal property. It will be important to check with your state's regulatory procedures, including county and local governance. You may also be required to apply for legal documents to secure home burial permissions.

Cremation allows for the indefinite housing of your remains without the necessity for burial or scattering of ashes. An assortment of decorative urns and wooden burial containment options can be purchased, usually sold through funeral homes.

Casket burial service based on a 2019 national average was $7,181. This fee for basic services includes embalming, preparation for viewing (if open casket service will be conducted), the use of funeral facility, funeral ceremony in lieu of church or fellowship services, transportation of casket, graveside service, and funeral director services. Basic costs do not include markers, a variety of memorial bereavement packages that include flowers, memorial cards, thank you notes, video memory maker, or additional family bereavement options.

Very basic cremation costs average $695. Basic cremation costs include removal of the remains, authorizations, use of the cremation casket, and basic staff services. This fee does not include the crematory fee or use of the facility or staff for any visitation or ceremony. Additional costs will include the cost of cremation urn, viewing and ceremony options, any legacy tributes or additional sentiment packages, or bereavement packages.

It is important to note that funeral home pricing varies state to state and individually. Consult the National Funeral Director Association at www.nfda.org for more detailed overview of funeral considerations, as well as Lincoln Heritage

Funeral Advantage (www.lhlic.com) for a wealth of funeral costs and information resource options.

Funeral Considerations

You will need to be aware and up to date regarding your state's regulations regarding death protocols. In most states, once death has been pronounced, the body is required to be interred within three days. A few states allow five days before a death must be pronounced with the exception of deaths requiring autopsy.

If an autopsy is to be performed, burial will commence once the medical examiner has issued the Death Certificate. This usually takes two weeks. If you have chosen to donate the remains for medical research, your family will receive your Death Certificate within four to six weeks with your cremated remains returned to your family six to twelve weeks after passing.

When cremation is chosen, there is no time constraint with regard to storage of the remains. In regards to cremation, there are few restrictions as to where ashes may be scattered. Before considering this option, check with your state's regulations regarding the dispersal of ashes. In some instances, written permission may be required for dispersal along shorelines or on government-owned properties.

There is a growing trend to conduct bedside home memorials following pronouncement of death. Before making a decision to conduct a home memorial, you need to be advised of state requirements regarding burials and be aware of physical decomposition following death. If you receive hospice vigil, the caretaker can prepare your body with scented oils to provide dignity for home viewing. This procedure would normally become the function of the emergency or funeral facility. Cremation or burial can commence following a home memorial.

A La Carte Sample Funeral Extended Expenditures

Consult www.nfda.or and www.lhlic.com for current pricing. Also note that costs vary state-to-state and by individual funeral homes.

Burial Choice

Use of Funeral Director and Staff	$2,000
Body Viewing Preparation	600
Viewing per Session	350
Cost of Casket	up to 14,000
Use of Funeral Facilities	500
Funeral Center Ceremony	550
Graveside Services	3,700
Gift Cards (expense per box)	$20
Memorial Book (per book design)	30
Prayer Cards (by designated number)	30-50
Life Memorial Video	300+

Cremation Choice

Use of Funeral Director and Staff	$2,000
Use of Funeral Facilities	500
Funeral Center Ceremony	550
Cremation Urn	up to 3,500
Gift Cards (expense per box)	$20
Memorial Book (per book design)	30
Prayer Cards (by designated number)	30-50
Life Memorial Video	300+

Discussing Personal Wishes

Even before you are faced with end-of-life planning, your personal final wishes need to be addressed. These can be awkward conversations that most family members do not want to discuss, but determining how to best carry out final wishes before any terminal diagnosis has been received will save much heartache. Topics of consideration may include:

• How do you prefer to be buried?
  Donate body to science for research
  Cremation
  Casket burial
  Where would you like to be buried?
  State, location, specific cemetery plot
  Ashes retained or scattered

• What type of life celebration ceremony would you like?
> Home ceremony
> Sanctuary
> Funeral hall
> Centrally located facility

• How would you like to be remembered?
> Life accomplishments
> Passionate goals
> Loving individual

• Who do you want at your bedside at the time of your transition?
> Closest family member(s)
> Closest friends
> Beloved pet

• Who would you like to be contacted after your passing?
> Relatives
> Friends
> Clubs/organizations

There may also be individuals you would like to make peace with before your transition. These conversations/ letters can be discussed/created with a mediator, doula practitioner, trusted faith-based administrator, or other interventional person who can make peace with any prior emotional compromise. In addition, mediator intervention can help to alleviate potential emotional compromise that may ensue between family members if conflict during life transition is anticipated.

This might also be time to discuss the possibility of recording or writing final memoirs. Technology is constantly changing but having a visual recording or written memoir may be a good way for your loved ones to remember you.

Organ Donation or Medical Research

Consideration may be entertained to donate your body to research after your passing. There are several agencies who can be contacted if this is of interest to you. There are a few restrictions with regard to eligibility. Exclusions exist in Arkansas, Minnesota, North Dakota, and New Jersey. Other exclusions include individuals experiencing communicative diseases such as HIV and Hepatitis, prolonged incarceration, or institutionalization, homelessness during the time of passing, severe over or under body weight, or a history of intravenous drug use. Generally all funeral expenses are covered including return of cremains, transportation of the body, and copies of death certification.

Creating a Letter of Instruction

*W*hile this category might seem unnecessary, it serves as an organized guide to direct those individuals who will handle your belongings and finalize obligations of your estate as to where your most important papers are located. This will also serve as follow-up reference to be sure your final wishes are honored. Consider the categories below that may provide easy guidance to settle any final accounting.

Listing Financial Accounting Institutions
See worksheet, page 98.
>> Banking institutes
>> Safety deposit box
>> Financial portfolios
>> Pensions
>> Annuities

Real estate holdings
Be sure you have a co-signer

Detail Where Important Papers are Kept
Bank account numbers/check books
Deeds, titles
Real estate
Auto
RV
Boat or other recreational vehicle
Other property
Pensions/annuities
Promissory notes/loans
Social security card
Birth certificate
Passport
Marriage license
Driver's license
Divorce decree
Immigration papers
Insurance policies

Section III

What to Do When Faced with a Terminal Illness

What to Do When Faced with a Terminal Illness

Getting a Second Opinion

The first thought after an initial diagnosis of a suspected terminal illness is shock, dismay, and a volley of uncertainty. It is important to take time to obtain a second or third opinion. Your caregiver/loved one may suggest this but take it upon yourself to research and explore all your options. Treatments may vary widely depending upon your specific diagnosis. In all scenarios, you must take action to treat your symptoms and make preparations for your care.

Discussing the Course of Illness

Determining Longevity

Now is the time to conduct a frank discussion with your caretaker/loved one on the expected longevity of your presenting symptoms. While no one can provide a precise time frame of your escalating diagnosis, your practitioner should be able to give you a time frame on which you can make plans to complete unfinished life accomplishments. This may include travel or completion of unfinished projects you have postponed. In the meantime, you will want to be prepared regarding the progression of your symptoms and the varying treatment options you may desire to incorporate into your treatment regimen.

What Symptoms May I Experience

Everyone is unique, but there are general patterns of symptom progression that can accompany the course of your particular diagnosis. You may chose not to be informed of potential symptoms, but often knowing what to expect may alleviate compacted stress and provide you more control of how to manage your progression. Ask direct questions of your practitioner to gain insight into the presentation of your symptomatology. See page 64 for further explanation of progressive symptomatology.

Discussing Treatment Options

When faced with a terminal prognosis, many considerations need to be addressed. You will want to discuss a variety of treatment options with your medical health practitioners. Potential medical interventions include:

Chemical intervention: If your physician suggests chemical intervention, you need to ask very specific questions concerning side effects, length of treatment, and the anticipated benefits. You will then need to weigh the treatment, side effects, cost association, and length of treatment against the quality of life and longevity of life this treatment option may afford.

Radiation: The use of radiation may reduce the size of a tumor or eradicate a localized area of concern. Both chemical and radiation treatments may cause uncomfortable or compromising side effects. Do not be afraid to ask your medical team exact questions to determine the benefit versus the length and discomfort that may accompany this treatment.

Surgical intervention: There are always risks with any surgery and there can be greater risks when your health is already compromised. But there may also be significant benefit to surgical intervention if a diseased area has been identified in its early stages. Discuss thoroughly your surgical and non-surgical options, as well as anticipated recovery length.

This section is not meant to replace your medical care but offer adjunct considerations to supplement traditional medical options.

Alternative considerations: There are a variety of alternative options that provide additional support measures during your care. Any modality that can support stress relief, relaxation, nutrition, and symptom relief will go a long way to enhancing your daily routines. Technical advances are improving treatment options, especially for individuals with terminal diagnoses. Some options are in their experimental phase, showing great promise in clinical trials. In the meantime, there are countless options to consider which may alter, improve, provide remission, promote well-being, and returned quality of life.

- Stem cell regeneration.

- Gene editing: While experimental and in its technical approval phase, CRISPR may well provide a cure to HIV, genetic diseases, and some cancers.

- Laser therapy: Using light frequencies set to your own body's frequency and the type of disease may provide comfort.

- Sound therapy: Using specific hertz frequencies attuned to your vibration and that of the specific disease has been noted in clinical trials to reverse or dismantle certain tumors.

- Meditation is not only soothing but can allow you to connect to your body's own healing mechanism. There are meditation apps that can be downloaded on electronic devices, meditation tapes, and online meditations designed to help you heal.

- Specialized massage therapy specifically designed for cancer patients can help to eliminate stress and promote relaxation as well as lymph drainage.

- Reflexology, can detoxify the body from the side effects of chemical and radiation treatments as well as provide stress release promoting beneficial relaxation and deep sleep.

- Acupuncture to realign broken energy circuits will provide momentary and often permanent relief from presenting symptoms.

- Emotional release techniques address causal factors and bring emotional balance back into existence.

- Nutritional support with dietary therapies and herbal supplements can be individually designed to your body to support healing benefits.

- Reiki energy therapies are gentle energetics designed to promote relaxation.

- Additional energy therapies designed to support disease processes that eliminate many side effects of medical treatment.

Preferred Options for Final Care

When presenting symptoms are no longer maintainable, you and your caretakers will need to determine which support measures will provide the best care for your pending needs. There are many options available to relieve family caretakers and provide for palliative care. Supplemental care may at first be intermittent. As care requirements progress, you may want to increase the frequency of palliative care.

- **Family caretakers** can be arranged to provide interim care within a home environment. Each care member can provide around the clock vigil as determined by everyone's schedule and needs.

- **Palliative caretakers** can be arranged to provide interim care on a routine basis. This may include hospice care, home health care or end-of-life doula care. These planned caretakers can perform monthly, weekly, daily, and finally 24-hour care.

- **Hospice** organizations provide nursing care, home health aides, social workers, chaplains, and vigil caretakers to ensure no individual dies alone. The advantage of hiring hospice care is to reduce out-of-pocket costs. The disadvantage to hiring hospice care can mean the denial of some diagnostic testing or hospitalization once hospice care has been initiated. Hospice caretakers/volunteers can provide initial medical resources and alert the family to watch for signs of declining viability. Hospice nursing personnel are able to administer pre-authorized prescriptions and provide medical intervention in coordination within prescribed medical directors in charge of your care. They are also available to answer questions regarding the individual's current health status if they have been given permission by a medical caregiver to do so.

- **Doula care** can provide emotional support, be an unbiased listener, engage in conversation, perform letter writing, organize personal papers, help coordinate final affairs, create sentiment packages, and conduct non-emotional discussions to determine final wishes. Doulas help create a desirable environment to surround you during the transition phase with important memories and assist in designing a sacred space during end-of-life care. In addition a doula can provide 24-hour vigil and bereavement consulting for family members.

- **Nursing care facilities** can be arranged to provide 24-hour care when home care is no longer a possibility.

"Death is the destination we all share. No one has ever escaped it. And that is as it should be because death is very likely the single best invention of life. It is life's change agent, it clears out the old to make way for the new."

– Steve Jobs

Final Preparations Before Transition

*N*o one is ever really ready to let their loved ones go, but you've done all the preliminary assembly of documentation and made peace with your life relationships. You're now preparing to enter a new chapter of your journey. Some questions may occur regarding potential presentation of end-of-life transition. More importantly questions may surface on what you may experience during your transition, what you may experience upon re-entry into the dimension of spirit, and how to reassure loved ones of your continuing presence throughout their lives after your physical departure.

Final Transition Indicators

After your initial diagnosis, your caretakers may have outlined the progression of your symptomatology. Every person will be different in the evolution of their specific physical presentations. Generally the individual will begin to conduct their own inward journey, coming to terms with their pending departure and being at ease with the process.

Months/Weeks Before Departure

Lethargy, lack of sustainable energy, and withdrawal from family or friends may be your initial behavioral presentation. Thought processes may seem scattered. Speech may be repetitive, perhaps distant. Cognitive behavior may be elusive. Physical changes may include reduced appetite and weight loss. At this time your body chemistry produces a mild euphoric sensation. What surrounding loved ones may witness may not be reflective of what you are experiencing.

One to Two Weeks Prior

Increased mental changes along with increased sleep may be apparent. Movements may seem erratic. Your body temperature may lower, circulation may become decreased, and the pulse may be irregular. You may notice increased perspiration. The skin at this time may be very fragile. Your skin color may change, especially noticeable around the lips or fingernails. You may experience increased lucid dreaming and may appear to be conducting conversation with invisible resources that may be coming to escort you into the next realm.

Days/Hours Before Transition

Muscle coordination may decrease; arms and hands may flail erratically. Speech may be more difficult and may stop altogether. Hands and feet may feel cold; the skin may be mottled, almost purple. There may be increased organ failure. Breathing may change, becoming more rapid or labored. Congestion may occur causing a rattling sound. The musculature is now relaxing causing fluid to collect around the heart and lungs. This can be highly disturbing for those keeping vigil during your final moments before transition. I am informed by medical personnel that this is more disturbing to those unfamiliar with the process than the physical symptoms you may be experiencing. Family may witness extreme relaxation or be present to apparent conversation between you and individuals from the spiritual realms coming to escort you into the next dimension.

Section IV

After Death Procedures

Information to
Share with Your
Loved Ones

After Death Procedures
Information to Share with Your Loved Ones

Out of State Death

If death occurs out of state, emergency personnel will notify family members and the local funeral home that has been designated to hold the body. The initial funeral home will coordinate with the funeral home in your location to arrange for transfer. Most funeral homes have working relationships with one another on behalf of family wishes.

Calling 911

If an individual is not under hospice care, the police will need to be notified immediately. The police will dispatch the medical examiner/coroner. If your family member is an organ donor, notify the emergency responders immediately so that proper protocols may be implemented on behalf of the wishes of your loved one. If your family member has decided to donate their body for medical research and has been accepted as a donor, indicate this to the emergency responders. The medical examiner/coroner will determine if further action following death will be necessary and coordinate further instruction to ancillary providers if organ donor or medical research protocols are to be initiated. The coroner/medical examiner must release the body before a funeral home, organ retriever, or medical research facility can do anything.

While EMS personnel generally cannot pronounce death, they will transport the individual to the nearest emergency facility where death can be affirmed by appropriate medical staff. The body will be held until the family authorizes the body to be released to a coroner or funeral official. The funeral home will then transport the body to the designated funeral home to await further instructions as delegated by the family.

Be sure to notify first responders if the individual is an organ donor or if the body is to be donated for medical research.

Keeping Death Orders Close at Hand

It will be important to be able to access special medical directives and have the contact information of key individuals who need to be notified immediately after transition. If authorized death orders cannot be accessed at time of death, emergency personnel may be obligated to perform resuscitation measures per their protocols of intervention. Knowing where these important papers are kept will alleviate much distress and prevent any miscommunication of the individual's final wishes.

Death in a Hospital/Nursing Care Facility

Staff at nursing care/hospital facilities will notify necessary authorities as well as family members immediately following death. If the family or individual has previously chosen a funeral home, the funeral home will be notified at the time of passing.

Who to Notify of Death

If the individual was under hospice care at the time of passing, the hospice caretaker will need to be notified. If hospice personnel were present during transition, the hospice caretaker will notify the proper authorities. If a doula representative was present at the time of transition they will also intervene on the family's behalf to notify the appropriate authorities of the individual's passing. Hospice/doula caretakers will provide further instruction to the family. Once emergency responders have been notified you will want to notify the individual's family physician, immediate family members, and/or designated individuals who will be important contributors during the initial phases of decision-making. After preliminary emergency responders have been notified and the coroner/medical examiner has released the body, you can contact the funeral home or instruct the medical care facility personnel to contact them on your behalf.

Who Can Pronounce Death?

While you may be observing your loved one initiate their final breath, there are protocols that according to state laws, must be observed. In addition there are procedures that can minimize the stress family members may endure after the expiration of their family member or friend. Each state varies on the individual(s) who may actually pronounce an individual as deceased. *Please refer to the reference section to find your state requirements.* (Table 90). In all states, a physician is listed as the one constant individual who can legally pronounce an individual as deceased and may also sign the Death Certificate. **All deaths, according to U.S. law must be declared within 48 hours of an individual's passing.**

Generally most EMS personnel cannot pronounce an individual as deceased. However, there are several states which allow advanced EMS or paramedic personnel to declare death. In most states, the medical examiner or coroner can pronounce and sign the Death Certificate.

The body will be held until the family authorizes the body to be released to a coroner or funeral official. The funeral home will then transport the body to the designated funeral home to await further instructions as delegated by the family.

Determining Need for Autopsy

If there is no explanation for the unexpected departure of your loved one, an autopsy may be necessary. The pronouncing physician, medical examiner, or approved personnel will make this decision. If an autopsy is necessary, the medical examiner will delay signing the Death Certificate until a primary diagnosis has been made. This can take up to two weeks.

Informing the Funeral Director

Once death protocols have been cleared by the proper authorities, it is now time to contact the funeral director. The funeral director will help to advise family members of funeral processes, transport the body from its holding facility, help coordinate selection of casket, and/or discuss cremation options if this has not already been determined. The funeral director will coordinate receipt of Death Certification on your behalf and help design a memorial service if this is desired. In addition, the funeral home staff will help with insurance company coordination and assist with all memorial arrangements. The goal is to relieve family members of as much stress as possible in dealing with the logistical impact of funeral planning.

Legal Death Protocols

With rare exception (e.g., need for autopsy), the **Death Certificate must be signed within 48 hours** of death and must be signed by the qualified professional. (See Reference Table I, page 90). The designated family member (executor of the estate) is provided with as many copies of the Death Certificate as necessary. This is an extremely important document. You will need to provide a copy of it to the IRS, Social

Security Department, and banking institution(s). In some cases, proof of transition will need to be provided to credit institutions, Veterans Affairs, and an assortment of proprietary companies (e.g., utilities, phone company, internet). Additional copies may be ordered at an additional cost. In many cases it is recommended that **10 copies** of the Death Certificate be secured to provide all inquiring vendors of the legal passing of your loved one. Your funeral home can obtain these on your behalf. See page 92 for a sample Death Certificate. Please note the death certificate can vary from state to state so becoming informed of your specific state's protocol ahead of time will be beneficial.

Financial Considerations

After services have concluded and you have received copies of the Death Certificates, you will now need to focus on notifying monthly recurring vendors, as well as any organization handling financial accounting on behalf of the deceased. Refer to page 101 for a contact worksheet with important numbers and passcodes of recurring vendors. It is likely each vendor will need verification of death by providing a copy of the Death Certificate.

If the deceased is a minor or young adult, many financial considerations may not need to be addressed. However, if the individual had any property holdings, decisions will need to be made regarding dispersal. Considerations regarding a private residence will need to be determined whether rental of property is more desirable than sale, or if there will be transfer of ownership.

Be sure to keep copies of all financial transactions, especially when considering IRS compilation. Consider having a CPA perform final accounting on behalf of your loved one, if the individual was of IRS reporting age. Additional support can be obtained by contacting **Social Security office at (800) 772-1213**. If your loved one has association with **Veterans Affairs** additional information can be obtained by contacting them at **(800) 827-1000**.

Residential Choices

If there is residential ownership and a choice to sell the property has been made, you will likely desire the expertise of a qualified agent to represent your interests during sale or transfer of ownership. If an estate is to be represented, there are organizations who can handle sale of entire estates.

You will need to notify the mortgage lender if a decision has been made to sell a residential property. You will still be responsible for the mortgage until transfer of title is made. If there is a homeowner's insurance agent(s), this vendor will also need to be notified unless the mortgage lender will handle notification on your behalf.

During property sale endeavors, you may want to keep utility accounts open until the residence is sold/ transferred. The service can either be discontinued or transferred to new owners once a sale has been negotiated.

Consult homeowner association if HOA or POA fees apply to a property.

In the case of rental housing, rental management will need to be notified. Again, you will want to notify the rental insurance agency of the individual's termination.

Vehicular Properties

If there is a balance on any vehicle or motorized property, you will need to notify each loan manager of the individual's passing. Property items may include car(s), motor home, boat, motorcycle, jet skis, etc. Each may require a copy of the Death Certificate. Designation of ownership or sale of any of these items can be made once determination to retain, purchase, or sell each item is made.

In addition to consideration of sale or transfer of title, you will need to be aware of state tax structures that will accompany yearly titles, along with any insurance that will accompany each individual vehicle.

Notifying Recurring Service Vendors

You will need to contact individual vendors to terminate services. In the case of credit services, all outstanding balances will need to be satisfied before the vendor will release obligation of repayment.

Investing portfolio managers will need to be contacted to alert them of the individual's passing. The financial advisor will more than likely have dispersal instructions that would

have previously been discussed at the origin of the portfolio investment. You will also want to notify any retirement
annuity provider. If there is a surviving spouse, pension inher-
itance may be an option. Your financial advisor can assist in
making arrangements for benefit transfer.

Portfolio investor
Social Security Administration
Veterans Affairs organization
Retirement provider
Automatic income depositor

Below is a general list of vendors that will require notification: See worksheet page 98.

Utilities
Electric
Gas
Water/sewer
Waste collection

Ancillary Vendors
Telephone (landline)
Mobile phone provider
Internet provider
Protection software provider
    Malwarebytes

    Norton

    LifeLock

Website provider (if applicable)

    GoDaddy

    Hostgator

    Other

Television provider –

    Cable, Netflix, Hulu, Roku, Amazon Fire

Insurance Vendors

Life insurance

Medical insurance

    Medicare (if applicable)

    Medicaid (if applicable)

    Prescription Recovery plans

Long-term care insurance

Disability vendor (Social Security)

Homeowners

Rental

    Automobile

    Boat

    Other recreational vehicle

Credit Lenders

You will want to immediately notify credit card vendors of the individual's passing. This will include all shopping/department store cards. Some familiar lenders may include:

Visa

MasterCard

American Express

Clothing stores

Hardware stores (Lowe's, Home Depot)

Shopping clubs (Sam's, Costco, BJ's)

Gas vendors (Exxon, Shell, BP)

The importance of notification of all credit vendors cannot be understated. It is unfortunate there would be those individuals who would take advantage of a deceased identification, but there is that potential. It will be important to change all passwords.

Charitable Contributions

You will want to know if the deceased contributed to any recurring charity. Charitable deductions have often been authorized to be automatic. Identifying individual vendors will stop automatic deductions. See Worksheet III, Page 104 to list charitable contributions. Sample charitable organizations include:

Wounded Warriors

St. Jude's Children

Shriner's Children

March of Dimes

Cancer Society

"Death is no more than passing from one room into another. But there's a difference for me, you know. Because in that other room I shall be able to see."

Helen Keller

Family Caretaking

*C*oping with the loss of a loved one is stressful enough without the added concern of determining who will take care of younger family members who may not understand the terminal process or who may be distracting to individuals coping with an array of decisions. In addition, details regarding elderly family members may also need to be addressed. Determining who you may call upon for interim short-and long-term care will be essential in helping you with immediate decision-making.

Resources: Reach out to ancillary providers to help with decisions that need to be made. This can include funeral homes, fellowship communities, or trusted friends. Medical personnel might also offer emotional support during this stressful transitional period.

Assigning Care for Spouse, Children, and Pets: There will be countless details needing attention. Foremost decisions will need to be made regarding longer term support/care of a spouse, parent, or child. Friends and family may lend immediate care but additional support can be arranged through community support organizations to assist in routines of daily functioning.

In addition to immediate family members, care of pets may also need to be designated. If it becomes necessary to re-home a beloved pet, humane shelters may advocate on behalf of a pet's care.

Memorial Services/ Home Memorial

*H*olding a memorial service is a personal preference. If a memorial service is chosen, has anyone been designated to write or give a eulogy? This could be the perfect moment to recognize your loved one's accomplishments, share memorable moments, or present memorable characteristics that will leave a lasting impression. Funeral directors and/or church officials can help personalize and coordinate a memorial service tailored specifically to family desires.

Home alters may provide a special memorial on behalf of your beloved family member. This may simply be a niche where you may place cremains, set a favorite picture remembrance, light a candle in memory, or provide fresh flowers.

Rumi indicates

"Goodbyes are only for those who love with their eyes. Because for those who love with heart and soul there is no such thing as separation."

Rumi lived from 1207 to 1273.

Family Bereavement

Death of a beloved individual can cause grief, anxiety, stress, depression, and uncertainty. Even if you have a strong family support system you may desire consultation with bereavement counselors, ministerial personnel, hospice individuals, or trained end-of-life doula consultants to listen to your concerns and if requested provide you with guidance and support to meet your family needs. Funeral homes are also expanding services to include an assortment of sentiment packages, compilation of life memoirs, and bereavement consultation. No matter what your belief, the natural process of grief can take a long time to process.

Often understanding the role all play in their life design helps to alleviate extended grief periods.

Life is a tapestry of events and interwoven interactions all designed to complement the soul's desire to evolve. Only when the final thread has been woven, is the tapestry complete. It is through much research that I can assert that only the physical representation of the beloved has departed. The soul exists with conscious awareness of all life activities and interactions within your personal and family life. Not one important gathering has been unattended. Not one voice of despair has gone unheard. Not one accomplishment has gone unnoticed. If you only knew who surrounded you with their loving embrace, you would never feel loneliness when missing t that personal hug from the individual you so treasured. Your beloved individual has merely stepped through a portal into another dimension of pure love and potential.

I wanted to share this excerpt from a message presented by Lee Carroll, as translated through **The Human Akash: A Discovery of the Blueprint Within** by Monika Muryani,"If you lose somebody you love, remember this: They may appear still and cold, but they are alive and well and looking at you, pleading with you to see the energy of love, that they are present. They are not gone."

The process of death is referred to as the "Wind of Transition." By the Creator's design, this is the way to call the individual home when their soul is needed elsewhere. Death is not an end but a new beginning.

When I'm Gone

When I come to the end of my journey
And I travel my last weary mile
Just forget if you can, that I ever frowned
And remember only the smile

Forget unkind words I have spoken
Remember some good I have done
Forget that I ever had heartache
And remember I've had loads of fun

Forget that I've stumbled and blundered
And sometimes fell by the way
Remember I have fought some hard battles
And won, ere the close of the day

Then forget to grieve for my going
I would not have you sad for a day
But in summer just gather some flowers
And remember the place where I lay

And come in the shade of evening
When the sun paints the sky in the west
Stand for a few moments beside me
And remember only my best.

by Mrs. Lyman Hancock

Section IV

*End-of-Life
Resource
Tables*

REFERENCE TABLE 1

State Legal Requirements/Pronouncement of Death

State	MD	PA	NP	RN	EMS	ME/ Coroner	Other
Alabama	X					X	
Alaska	X				X	X	
Arizona	X	X				X	
Arkansas	X					X	
California	X			X	X	X	
Colorado	X						
Connecticut	X			X (Can sign Death Certificate)			
Delaware	X					X	
Florida	X	X		X		X	
Georgia	X			X			
Hawaii	X			X			
Idaho	X					X	
Illinois	X					X	
Indiana	X				X		
Iowa			X	X	X	X	
Kansas	X	X	X				
Kentucky	X	X			X	X	X Chiropractor
Louisiana	X						
Maine	X	X	X				
Maryland	X				X	X	
Massachusetts	X						
Michigan	X			X			
Minnesota	X	X	X	X		X	
Mississippi	X					X	
Missouri	X	X	X	X		X	
Montana	X		X	X			
Nebraska	X						
Nevada	X					X	

State	MD	PA	NP	RN	EMS	ME/Coroner	Other
New Hampshire		X					X
New Jersey		X	X				X
New Mexico		X			X		
New York		X		X	X		X
North Carolina		X	X		X		X
North Dakota		X					X
Ohio		X	X		X		Chiropractor
Oklahoma		X					X
Oregon		X		X	X		X
Pennsylvania		X	X	X	X		X
Rhode Island		X					
South Carolina		X					X
South Dakota		X		X	X		
Tennessee		X			X		X
Texas		X			X	(Can pronounce by phone)	
Utah		X					X
Vermont		X	X				X
Virginia		X				X	X
Washington		X	X	X	X	X	
West Virginia		X	X		X		
Wisconsin		X					X
Wyoming		X	X	X			

REFERENCE TABLE 2
Sample U.S. Standard Death Certificate

U.S. STANDARD CERTIFICATE OF DEATH LOCAL FILE NO. STATE FILE NO. 1. DECEDENT'S LEGAL NAME (Include AKA's if any) (First, Middle, Last) 2. SEX 3. SOCIAL SECURITY NUMBER 4a. AGE-Last Birthday 4b. UNDER 1 YEAR 4c. UNDER 1 DAY (Years) Months Days Hours Minutes 5. DATE OF BIRTH (Mo/Day/Yr) 6. BIRTHPLACE (City and State or Foreign Country) 7a. RESIDENCE-STATE 7b. COUNTY 7c. CITY OR TOWN 7d. STREET AND NUMBER 7e. APT. NO. 7f. ZIP CODE 7g. INSIDE CITY LIMITS? ☐ Yes ☐ No 8. EVER IN US ARMED FORCES? ☐ Yes ☐ No 9. MARITAL STATUS AT TIME OF DEATH ☐ Married ☐ Married, but separated ☐ Widowed ☐ Divorced ☐ Never Married ☐ Unknown 10. SURVIVING SPOUSE'S NAME (If wife, give name prior to first marriage) 11. FATHER'S NAME (First, Middle, Last) 12. MOTHER'S NAME PRIOR TO FIRST MARRIAGE (First, Middle, Last) 13a. INFORMANT'S NAME 13b. RELATIONSHIP TO DECEDENT 13c. MAILING ADDRESS (Street and Number, City, State, Zip Code) 14. PLACE OF DEATH (Check only one: see instructions) IF DEATH OCCURRED IN A HOSPITAL: ☐ Inpatient ☐ Emergency Room/Outpatient ☐ Dead on Arrival IF DEATH OCCURRED SOMEWHERE OTHER THAN A HOSPITAL: ☐ Hospice facility ☐ Nursing home/Long term care facility ☐ Decedent's home ☐ Other (Specify): 15. FACILITY NAME (If not institution, give street & number) 16. CITY OR TOWN , STATE, AND ZIP CODE 17. COUNTY OF DEATH 18. METHOD OF DISPOSITION: ☐ Burial ☐ Cremation ☐ Donation ☐ Entombment ☐ Removal from State ☐ Other (Specify):_____
19. PLACE OF DISPOSITION (Name of cemetery, crematory, other place) 20. LOCATION-CITY, TOWN, AND STATE 21. NAME AND COMPLETE ADDRESS OF FUNERAL FACILITY NAME OF DECEDENT _____
_____ For use by physician or institution To Be Completed/ Verified By: FUNERAL DIRECTOR: 22. SIGNATURE OF FUNERAL SERVICE LICENSEE OR OTHER AGENT 23. LICENSE NUMBER (Of Licensee) ITEMS 24-28 MUST BE COMPLETED BY PERSON WHO PRONOUNCES OR CERTIFIES DEATH 24. DATE PRONOUNCED DEAD (Mo/Day/Yr) 25. TIME PRONOUNCED DEAD 26. SIGNATURE OF PERSON PRONOUNCING DEATH (Only when applicable) 27. LICENSE NUMBER 28. DATE SIGNED (Mo/Day/Yr) 29. ACTUAL OR PRESUMED DATE OF DEATH (Mo/Day/Yr) (Spell Month) 30. ACTUAL OR PRESUMED TIME OF DEATH 31. WAS MEDICAL EXAMINER OR CORONER CONTACTED? ☐ Yes ☐ No CAUSE OF DEATH (See instructions and examples) 32. PART I. Enter the chain of events--diseases, injuries, or complications--that directly caused the death. DO NOT enter terminal events such as cardiac arrest, respiratory arrest,

or ventricular fibrillation without showing the etiology. DO NOT ABBREVIATE. Enter only one cause on a line. Add additional lines if necessary. IMMEDIATE CAUSE (Final disease or condition ---------> a._____

_____ resulting in death) Due to (or as a consequence of): Sequentially list conditions, b._____
_____ if any, leading to the cause Due to (or as a consequence of): listed on line a. Enter the UNDERLYING CAUSE c._____
_____ (disease or injury that Due to (or as a consequence of): initiated the events resulting in death) LAST d._____
_____ A pproximate interval: Onset to death _____ _____ _____
_____ 33. WAS AN AUTOPSY PERFORMED? ☐ Yes ☐ No PART II. Enter other significant conditions contributing to death but not resulting in the underlying cause given in PART I 34. WERE AUTOPSY FINDINGS AVAILABLE TO COMPLETE THE CAUSE OF DEATH? ☐ Yes ☐ No 35. DID TOBACCO USE CONTRIBUTE TO DEATH? ☐ Yes ☐ Probably ☐ No ☐ Unknown 36. IF FEMALE: ☐ Not pregnant within past year ☐ Pregnant at time of death ☐ Not pregnant, but pregnant within 42 days of death ☐ Not pregnant, but pregnant 43 days to 1 year before death ☐ Unknown if pregnant within the past year 37. MANNER OF DEATH ☐ Natural ☐ Homicide ☐ Accident ☐ Pending Investigation ☐ Suicide ☐ Could not be determined 38. DATE OF INJURY (Mo/Day/Yr) (Spell Month) 39. TIME OF INJURY 40. PLACE OF INJURY (e.g., Decedent's home; construction site; restaurant; wooded area) 41. INJURY AT WORK? ☐ Yes ☐ No 42. LOCATION OF INJURY: State: City or Town: Street & Number: Apartment No.: Zip Code: 43. DESCRIBE HOW INJURY OCCURRED: 44. IF TRANSPORTATION INJURY, SPECIFY: ☐ Driver/Operator ☐ Passenger ☐ Pedestrian ☐ Other (Specify) 45. CERTIFIER (Check only one): ☐ Certifying physician-To the best of my knowledge, death occurred due to the cause(s) and manner stated. ☐ Pronouncing & Certifying physician-To the best of my knowledge, death occurred at the time, date, and place, and due to the cause(s) and manner stated. ☐ Medical Examiner/ Coroner-On the basis of examination, and/or investigation, in my opinion, death occurred at the time, date, and place, and due to the cause(s) and manner stated. Signature of cer-

State Burial and Cremation Costs
Reference Table 3
(Based on 2018 Estimates)

State	Average Burial	Lowest Cremation
Alabama	$10,000	$895
Alaska	1,000-5,000	1,500-3,000
Arizona	7,045	639
Arkansas	8,755	695
California	7,045	625
Colorado	7,000	500
Connecticut	6,000	2,200
Delaware	7,045	999
Florida	7,755	500
Georgia	7,755	1,400
Hawaii	7,000	985
Idaho	7,045	695
Illinois	7,045	1,000
Indiana	2,795	985
Iowa	2,620	1,095
Kansas	5,814	695
Kentucky	5,000	795
Louisiana	7,045	1,550
Maine	7,045	695
Maryland	7,045	875
Massachusetts	7,181	1,395
Michigan	7,181	220
Minnesota	7,300	600
Mississippi	7,045	995
Missouri	7,000	695
Montana	7,000	695
Nebraska	7,181	990
Nevada	7,000	595
New Hampshire	4,000	1,295
New Jersey	7,755	3,500
New Mexico	7,045	695
New York	8,000	495

State Burial and Cremation Costs
Reference Table 3
(Based on 2018 Estimates)

State	Average Burial	Lowest Cremation
North Carolina	7,755	3,000
North Dakota	1,000	695
Ohio	7,045	699
Oklahoma	2,895	895
Oregon	895-2,965	595
Pennsylvania	7,181	695
Rhode Island	1,850	895
South Carolina	7,755	695
South Dakota	2,375	695
Tennessee	7,775	995
Texas	7,755	595
Utah	7,045	750
Vermont	7.045	695
Virginia	7,045	1,400
Washington	7,045	699
West Virginia	4,595	1,125
Wisconsin	7,045	995
Wyoming	8,350	695

Bibliography Resources

Books

Michael Dooley: *The Top Ten Things Dead People Want to Tell You*
Dr. Bruce Lipton: *Biology of Belief*
Dr. Raymond Moody: *Life after Life*
Dr. Michael Newton: *Journey of Souls; Life between Life*
Dr. Kubler- Ross : *On Death and Dying*
Dr. Brian Weiss: *Many Lives, Many Masters*
Lee Carroll/Monika Muryani: *The Human Akash*
Dr. Eben Alexander: *Proof of Heaven; A Neurosurgeon's Journey into the Afterlife*

Great Websites

www.FormsSwift.com
www.LawDepot.com
www.MedCure.org
www.OKtoDie.com
www.verywellhealth.com
UCSF Medical Center

Koch Funeral Consultants
Monroe Institute
U.S. CDC
www.secretary.state.nc.us/ahcdr/forms.aspx.5
State Death Protocol websites
State Legal Requirements/IRS Compliance

www.consumerreports.org/what-to-do-when-a-loved-one-dies
https://cremationinstitute.com
www.informationnow.org
www.legalvoice.org
www.lhlic.com (Lincoln Heritage Funeral Advantage)
www.nfda.org (National Funeral Director Association)
www.nolo.com/legal-encyclopedia/burial-cremation-laws-north-carolina
www.ucsfhealth.org/education/bereavement

END-OF-LIFE PLANNING WORKSHEETS

Emergency Numbers

Emergency Center   911

Physician _____   (___) _____

Hospice Center   (___) _____

Clergy_____   (___) _____

Funeral Home   (___) _____

Family Members

_____   (___) _____

_____   (___) _____

_____   (___) _____

_____   (___) _____

_____   (___) _____

_____   (___) _____

Other

_____   (___) _____

_____   (___) _____

_____   (___) _____

List Recurring Bills and Contact Information
Worksheet I

Vendor	Account #	Contact Information

List Recurring Bills and Contact Information Worksheet I

Vendor	Account #	Contact Information
_____	_____	_____
_____	_____	_____
_____	_____	_____
_____	_____	_____
_____	_____	_____
_____	_____	_____
_____	_____	_____
_____	_____	_____
_____	_____	_____
_____	_____	_____
_____	_____	_____
_____	_____	_____
_____	_____	_____
_____	_____	_____
_____	_____	_____

List Recurring Bills and Contact Information Worksheet I

Vendor	Account #	Contact Information
_____	_____	_____
_____	_____	_____
_____	_____	_____
_____	_____	_____
_____	_____	_____
_____	_____	_____
_____	_____	_____
_____	_____	_____
_____	_____	_____
_____	_____	_____
_____	_____	_____
_____	_____	_____
_____	_____	_____
_____	_____	_____
_____	_____	_____
_____	_____	_____

List of Accounts and Passwords
Worksheet II

Vendor   **Account #**

_____   _____

User Name_____   Password _____
Telephone _____

_____   _____

User Name_____   Password _____
Telephone _____

_____   _____

User Name_____   Password _____
Telephone _____

_____   _____

User Name_____   Password _____
Telephone _____

_____   _____

User Name_____   Password _____
Telephone _____

_____   _____

User Name_____   Password _____
Telephone _____

List of Accounts and Passwords
Worksheet II

Vendor   **Account #**

_____   _____

User Name_____   Password _____
Telephone _____

_____   _____

User Name_____   Password _____
Telephone _____

_____   _____

User Name_____   Password _____
Telephone _____

_____   _____

User Name_____   Password _____
Telephone _____

_____   _____

User Name_____   Password _____
Telephone _____

_____   _____

User Name_____   Password _____
Telephone _____

List of Accounts and Passwords
Worksheet II

Vendor   **Account #**

_____   _____

User Name_____   Password _____
Telephone _____

_____   _____

User Name_____   Password _____
Telephone _____

_____   _____

User Name_____   Password _____
Telephone _____

_____   _____

User Name_____   Password _____
Telephone _____

_____   _____

User Name_____   Password _____
Telephone _____

_____   _____

User Name_____   Password _____
Telephone _____

Charitable Contribution
Worksheet III

Charity   **Account #**   **Contact Number**

_____   _____   _____

_____   _____   _____

_____   _____   _____

_____   _____   _____

_____   _____   _____

_____   _____   _____

_____   _____   _____

_____   _____   _____

_____   _____   _____

_____   _____   _____

_____   _____   _____

_____   _____   _____

_____   _____   _____

Family/Friend Contact Information Worksheet IV

Family/Friend _____

Telephone # _____

Address _____

_____State _____ Zip _____

Family/Friend _____

Telephone # _____

Address _____

_____State _____ Zip _____

Family/Friend _____

Telephone # _____

Address _____

_____State _____ Zip _____

Family/Friend _____

Telephone # _____

Address _____

_____State _____ Zip _____

Family/Friend Contact Information
Worksheet IV

Family/Friend _____

Telephone # _____

Address _____

_____State _____ Zip _____

Family/Friend _____

Telephone # _____

Address _____

_____State _____ Zip _____

Family/Friend _____

Telephone # _____

Address _____

_____State _____ Zip _____

Family/Friend _____

Telephone # _____

Address _____

_____State _____ Zip _____

Family/Friend Contact Information Worksheet IV

Family/Friend _____

Telephone # _____

Address _____

_____State _____ Zip _____

Family/Friend _____

Telephone # _____

Address _____

_____State _____ Zip _____

Family/Friend _____

Telephone # _____

Address _____

_____State _____ Zip _____

Family/Friend _____

Telephone # _____

Address _____

_____State _____ Zip _____

Meet Jilliana Raymond

AUTHOR, SPEAKER, VISIONARY, JILLIANA RAYMOND, has been introducing individuals to the spiritual stewards who watch over us through her writing and teaching for over twenty-five years. Her personal quest to understand the universal energy components that impact our daily lives began when she encountered her own intensely difficult life challenges. Her research has led her to the discoveries she distills through her works and that she shares with her audiences.

Jilliana is an international, award-winning author and national radio guest distilling her discoveries into powerful principles for living. Through her writing, transformational workshops, and her private consultations, she promotes a greater understanding of the language and teachings of our spiritual universe to empower each of us individually and globally.

In addition, Jilliana is trained in multiple therapeutic modalities, and developed her own powerfully transformational National Board of Massage Reflexology Protocol: Integrated Sole Energy Therapy (ISET). To schedule an event, contact Jilliana Raymond at:

jillianaraymond@gmail.com

www.jillianaraymond.com

Additional Titles Available on Amazon:

New Beginnings
Powerful Principles for Transformation
If you knew everything you do in your life matters, would you change anything? Earth's inhabitants are undergoing a period of balancing. Anything that is no longer complimentary to your life is undergoing change. How will this change affect you? New Beginnings challenges complex life issues and invites its readers to alleviate restrictive life patterns while aligning with a new vision for an evolving world. Get your copy today and discover the changing life values that will enhance your living experience.

The New Covenants:
An exploration into the spiritual laws that govern our individual living
Over 3,000 years ago a set of commandments was issued to provide guidance and structure to a chaotic society. Humanity is once again immersed in chaos and on the threshold of creating an evolving world. It is time to provide a new set of directives to provide a new life template so all can experience the life they are born to live.

Life is a Spiritual Soup
offers insight into global dynamic change. Never before has humanity faced more challenges, as mankind is experiencing its fragility and is being brought together to experience its oneness. *Life Is a Spiritual Soup* offers a working definition in the meaning of spirituality and explains that spirituality is how one expresses their unique life journey, not how one expresses their religious choice. Jilliana reminds us that not only are we responsible for what we attract in our life but through our projected thought we are creating the future events of our living experience.

Made in the USA
Columbia, SC
29 August 2019